Harcourt
SOCIAL Studies

Arizona Connections
Grade 2

Harcourt
SCHOOL PUBLISHERS

www.harcourtschool.com

Series Author

Dr. Tyrone C. Howard
Associate Professor
UCLA Graduate School of Education
& Information Studies
University of California at Los
Angeles
Los Angeles, California

Classroom Reviewers and Contributors

Ginny Biddle
Teacher
Country Place Elementary School
Tolleson, Arizona

Garrie S. Doss
Teacher
Dobson Academy
Chandler, Arizona

Evelynn Drogg
Teacher
Carol Rae Ranch Elementary School
Gilbert, Arizona

Rachel Ernst
Teacher
Country Place Elementary School
Tolleson, Arizona

Vicki Geiger
Teacher
Cholla Middle School
Phoenix, Arizona

Linda Gering
Apache Junction Unified School
District
Apache Junction, Arizona

Tonya Hopkins
Teacher
Dobson Academy
Chandler, Arizona

Karen Lee-Price
Lakeview Elementary School
Phoenix, Arizona

Mary Stuewe
Professional Learning Specialist
Tuscon Unified School District
Tuscon, Arizona

Sue Wahlund
Media Specialist
Canyon Rim Elementary School
Mesa, Arizona

Harcourt
SCHOOL PUBLISHERS

Maps
researched and prepared by

Printed in the United States of America

ISBN-13: 978-0-15-356254-9
ISBN-10: 0-15-356254-4

3 4 5 6 7 8 9 10 073 14 13 12 11 10 09 08 07

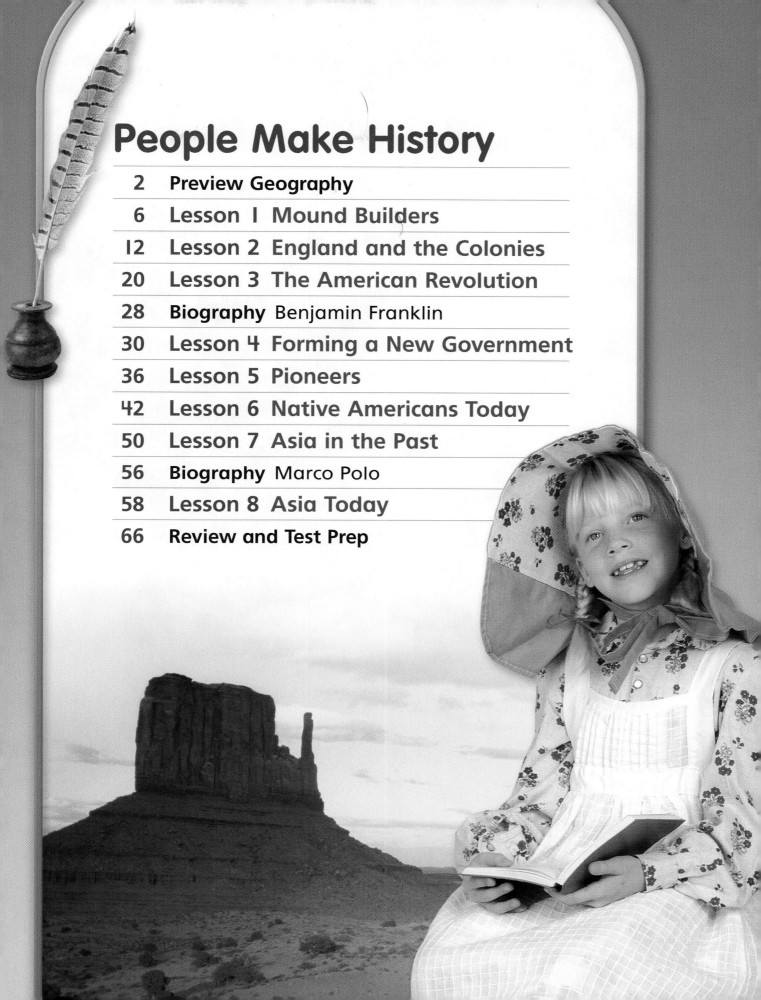

People Make History

People Make History

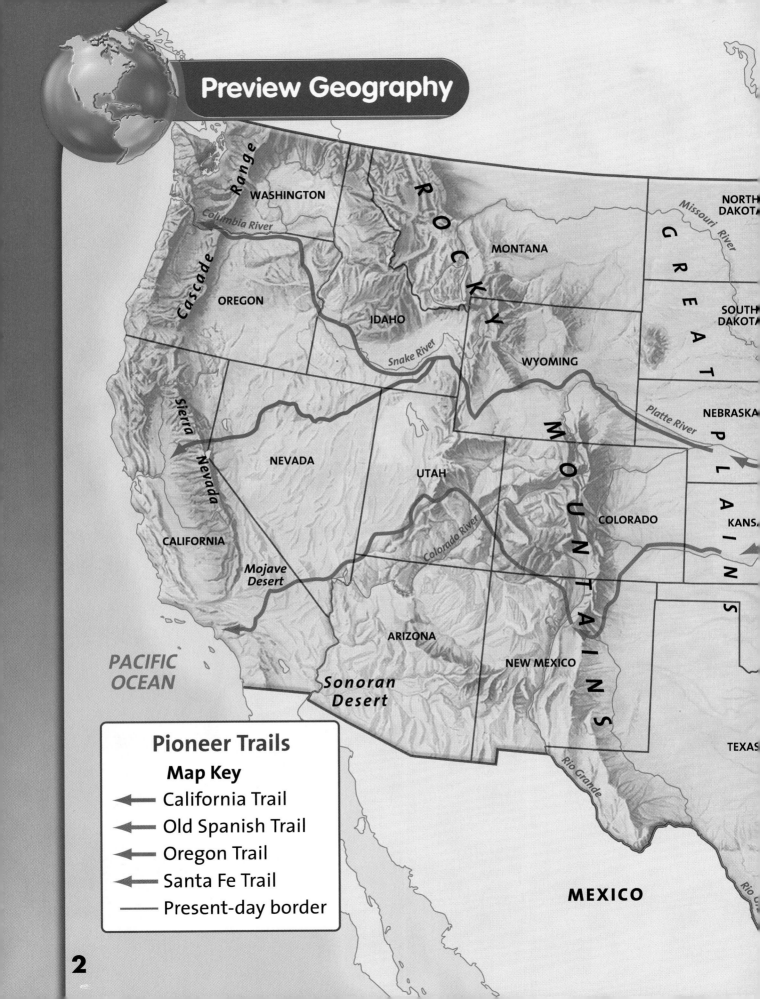

Preview Geography

WASHINGTON
Cascade Range
Columbia River
OREGON
Sierra Nevada
NEVADA
CALIFORNIA
Mojave Desert
PACIFIC OCEAN
ARIZONA
Sonoran Desert
IDAHO
Snake River
MONTANA
WYOMING
UTAH
Colorado River
COLORADO
NEW MEXICO
Rio Grande
ROCKY MOUNTAINS
NORTH DAKOTA
SOUTH DAKOTA
NEBRASKA
KANSAS
TEXAS
GREAT PLAINS
Missouri River
Platte River
MEXICO

Pioneer Trails

Map Key

← California Trail
← Old Spanish Trail
← Oregon Trail
← Santa Fe Trail
— Present-day border

2

CANADA

MINNESOTA

Lake Superior

WISCONSIN

MICHIGAN

Lake Michigan

Lake Huron

Mississippi River

IOWA

ILLINOIS

INDIANA

OHIO

Lake Ontario

Lake Erie

NEW
YORK

PENNSYLVANIA

VERMONT

MAINE

NEW
HAMPSHIRE

MASSACHUSETTS

RHODE ISLAND

CONNECTICUT

NEW JERSEY

DELAWARE

MARYLAND

Missouri River

MISSOURI

KENTUCKY

Ohio River

WEST
VIRGINIA

VIRGINIA

APPALACHIAN MOUNTAINS

NORTH
CAROLINA

OKLAHOMA

Arkansas River

ARKANSAS

Mississippi River

TENNESSEE

SOUTH
CAROLINA

MISSISSIPPI

ALABAMA

GEORGIA

LOUISIANA

ATLANTIC
OCEAN

FLORIDA

North

West

East

South

Gulf of Mexico

3

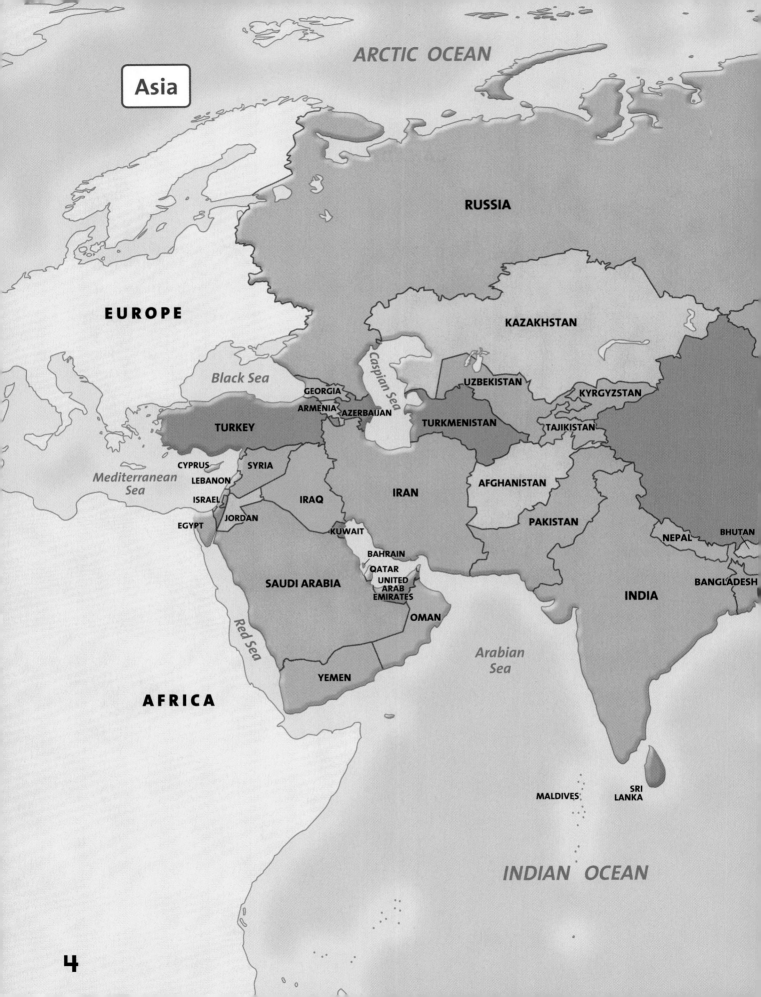

Asia

ARCTIC OCEAN

RUSSIA

EUROPE

KAZAKHSTAN

Black Sea

Caspian Sea

GEORGIA

UZBEKISTAN

KYRGYZSTAN

ARMENIA

AZERBAIJAN

TURKMENISTAN

TAJIKISTAN

TURKEY

CYPRUS

SYRIA

Mediterranean
Sea

LEBANON

IRAN

AFGHANISTAN

ISRAEL

IRAQ

EGYPT

JORDAN

PAKISTAN

NEPAL

BHUTAN

KUWAIT

BAHRAIN

BANGLADESH

QATAR

SAUDI ARABIA

UNITED
ARAB
EMIRATES

INDIA

OMAN

Red Sea

Arabian
Sea

YEMEN

AFRICA

SRI
LANKA

MALDIVES

INDIAN OCEAN

4

ARCTIC OCEAN

RUSSIA

Bering Sea

Sea of Okhotsk

MONGOLIA

NORTH KOREA

Sea of Japan

SOUTH KOREA

JAPAN

CHINA

North

West — East

South

MYANMAR (BURMA)

TAIWAN

PACIFIC OCEAN

LAOS

Philippine Sea

THAILAND

VIETNAM

CAMBODIA

PHILIPPINES

BRUNEI

MALAYSIA

SINGAPORE

INDONESIA

EAST TIMOR

5

Lesson 1

Mound Builders

 What to Know
Who were the
first people living in
North America?

Vocabulary
archaeologist
artifact

Look at this hill. Can you tell that it was made by people? It was built by Mound Builders a very long time ago. The Mound Builders were people who piled up layers of earth to make mounds. Where did the Mound Builders live? Why did they build mounds?

Miamisburg Mound

Searching for Clues

These are the kinds of questions I ask every day. I look for clues! I am an archaeologist. An **archaeologist** is a scientist who studies things left behind by people long ago.

Sometimes I find small pieces of animal bones near a mound. These are important clues. They tell me what kind of food the people ate. The best clues, though, are things I find inside the mounds.

Reading Check What are mounds?

Digging Up the Past

My job is to dig in the mounds for artifacts. An **artifact** is any object, big or small, that people have made. If I am lucky, I might find a pot, a tool, or even a toy. Each artifact I find adds to what we know about the Mound Builders.

The first people living in what is now the United States were Native Americans. Some Native American groups built mounds in different parts of the country. One early group, the Adena, built mounds in which they buried their dead. They left gifts with the dead for them to use in another life.

An Adena artifact

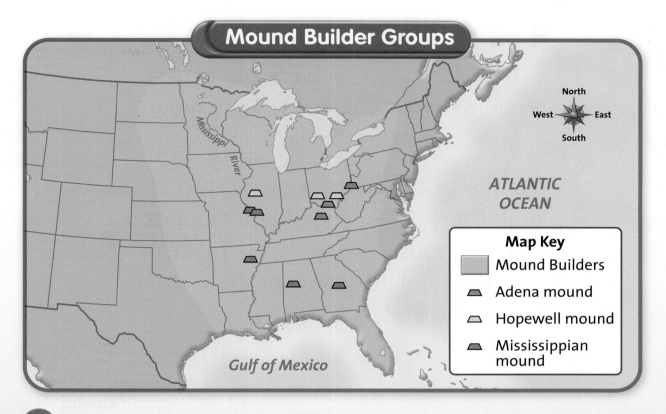

Mound Builder Groups

Map Key
- Mound Builders
- Adena mound
- Hopewell mound
- Mississippian mound

ATLANTIC OCEAN

Gulf of Mexico

Mississippi River

North, West, East, South

MAP SKILL Which mound-building group built mounds the farthest south?

The Hopewell, a later group, buried the ashes of their dead in mounds. Artifacts show that these people traded with other communities. Their gifts for the dead were often made from things such as shells, shark teeth, and silver.

Reading Check Why are the mounds themselves artifacts?

A Hopewell artifact

9

Rise and Fall

The Mississippians were the largest group of Mound Builders. They grew crops to feed themselves.

Some of the Mississippians lived in large cities. They made large mounds with flat tops. On top of the mounds, they built big buildings for their important leaders.

A Mississippian mound

Over time, the mound-building communities disappeared. They left behind many clues about their history.

Today archaeologists try to put these clues together to solve the mystery of the Mound Builders.

Reading Check **What happened to the three communities of Mound Builders?**

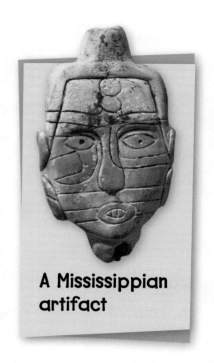
A Mississippian artifact

Summary The first people living in North America were Native Americans. Some early Native Americans were Mound Builders.

Review

① **What to Know** Who were the first people living in North America?

② **Vocabulary** Name a classroom **artifact** that future archaeologists might discover.

③ ✏ **Write** Write three facts you learned about the Mound Builders.

④ **Compare and Contrast** How are the mounds of the Mississippians different from those of the other two groups?

11

England and the Colonies

What to Know
How did early American colonists live?

Vocabulary

trade

merchant

Settlers came from Europe to make new homes in the colonies. The people who lived in these colonies were colonists. One way to learn about their lives is by reading letters like these written to their families and friends.

The settlers sailed across the ocean on ships.

Virginia, 1607

My dearest family,

We have made it to the new land. There are people here called Powhatans. We do not speak the same language as one another. However, we have learned to talk to each other in different ways.

We are always pleased to **trade**, or exchange, goods with the Powhatans. I have become a successful merchant in our colony. As a **merchant**, I trade many goods with the Powhatans and with the other colonists.

Love,
John

Merchants traded goods with Native Americans.

13

Massachusetts, 1621

Dearest brother,

We are looking forward to a good harvest this season. We could not have done it without our Wampanoag friends. They helped us clear the land and plant our crops.

If the harvest is as good as we hope it will be, we will celebrate with wild turkey, fish, fruits, and vegetables!

Love,
Eleanor

Settlers grew new kinds of crops in the colonies.

Virginia, 1735

Dearest Grandmama,

I am to finish school next year. Father says he is willing to send me to college in England. You will have your oldest grandson near you!

Little Judith will be going to school next year. That is also very exciting. Mother has told us about when she went to school. She was lucky, she says. Girls did not often get to go to school then.

Your loving grandson,
Thomas

Children read from hornbooks.

Children went to school in the colonies.

New Hampshire, 1758

My dearest Hannah,

   We have found a good place to settle here. We have a very nice farm. We have also made many new friends. Last week, all the men and boys from nearby came to help us build our barn.

   The women cooked and baked. When the work was done, we all sat down to a feast. It was a wonderful time!

Warmest wishes to all.

Your brother,
James

Colonists worked together to build barns.

Rhode Island, 1765

My good friend Martin,

What an unhappy time this is! Our latest problem is the Stamp Act. The king of England wants to raise money from us to pay for his army to be here. Many people are angry about this law.

People say they will not buy anything else that comes from England. This will be hard for you, my friend. You will have to find other places to sell your goods.

Your friend,
William Smith

No Stamp Act!

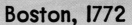
Boston, 1772

Dear Ann,

Last week, hundreds of chests of tea arrived from England on three ships. It was an unhappy sight.

Many people are angry with the king's new law on tea. Merchants are allowed to sell tea only from England. Some colonists have quit drinking tea!

Last night, about 200 men dressed as Indians went on board the ships.

They broke open the chests of tea and dumped them over the sides of the ships. I am sure more trouble will come from this.

Your cousin,
Franklin

Summary Colonists lived in the colonies. They traded goods, attended school, and worked together. Many colonists were unhappy with the king's laws.

Review

1. **What to Know** How did early American colonists live?

2. **Vocabulary** What does it mean to **trade**?

3. **Write** Suppose you were at the Boston Tea Party. Write a journal entry that describes how you felt that night.

4. **Recall and Retell** Each letter in this lesson tells something about things that happened in the colonies. Choose one letter, and draw a picture that shows what happened. Label your drawing.

19

Lesson 3

What to Know
How did our country become independent?

Vocabulary
revolution

The American Revolution

A reporter from a local newspaper has been able to go back in time. She interviews people about the American Revolution.

The Shot Heard Around the World

REPORTER People talk about the shot heard around the world. What was that?

MINUTEMAN That was the first shot fired in the American Revolution.

REPORTER What is a revolution?

MINUTEMAN A **revolution** is a sudden change in the way people think and act. People wanted to make a change in our government. They had to fight to do that.

REPORTER Where were the first battles of the American Revolution fought?

MINUTEMAN They took place in Lexington and Concord, towns in Massachusetts, on April 19, 1775. The Minutemen were all there.

REPORTER Who were the Minutemen?

MINUTEMAN They were mostly farmers ready to fight the English at a minute's warning.

REPORTER How did you know when the English were coming?

MINUTEMAN You should probably ask Paul Revere that question.

REPORTER Thank you, I'll do that.

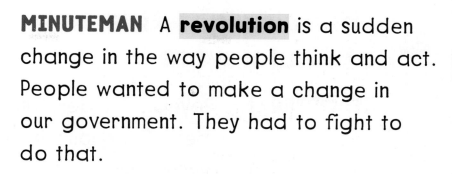

The Midnight Ride of Paul Revere

REPORTER Mr. Revere, I understand that you were a member of a group in Boston. What was that group called?

PAUL REVERE The group was called the Sons of Liberty. I rode a horse and carried messages for them.

REPORTER You were carrying a message on April 18, 1775. What was that message?

PAUL REVERE It was a message to tell the Sons of Liberty and the Minutemen that the English were coming.

REPORTER Did you get the message to them?

PAUL REVERE Yes.

REPORTER What happened then?

PAUL REVERE The Minutemen were waiting for the British in Lexington the next morning. The American Revolution had begun!

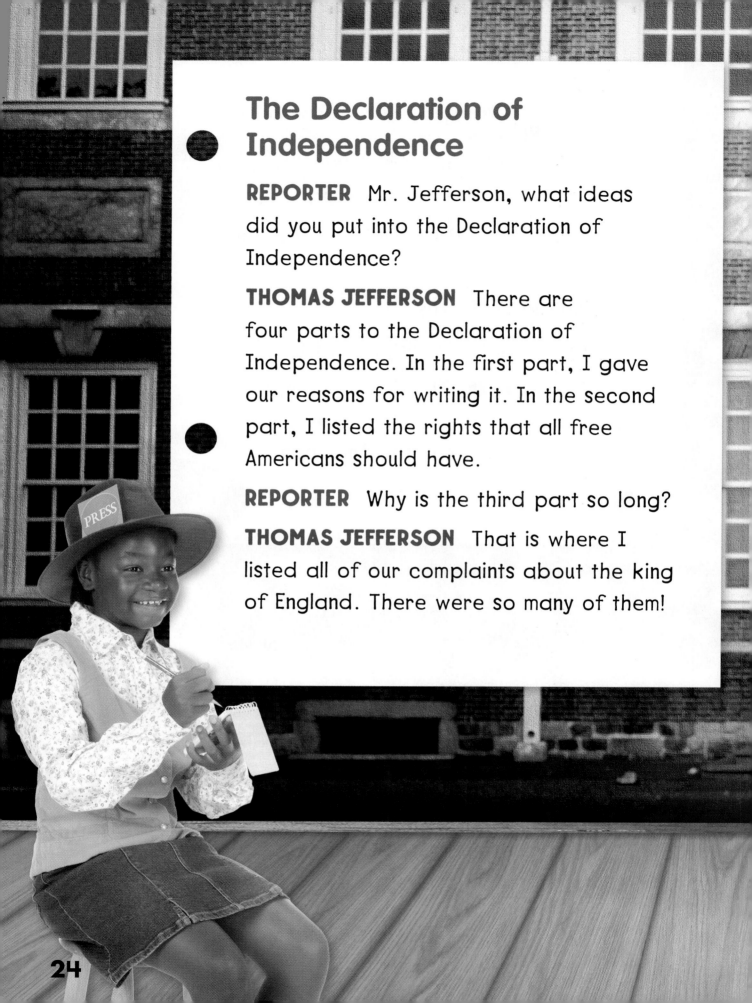

The Declaration of Independence

REPORTER Mr. Jefferson, what ideas did you put into the Declaration of Independence?

THOMAS JEFFERSON There are four parts to the Declaration of Independence. In the first part, I gave our reasons for writing it. In the second part, I listed the rights that all free Americans should have.

REPORTER Why is the third part so long?

THOMAS JEFFERSON That is where I listed all of our complaints about the king of England. There were so many of them!

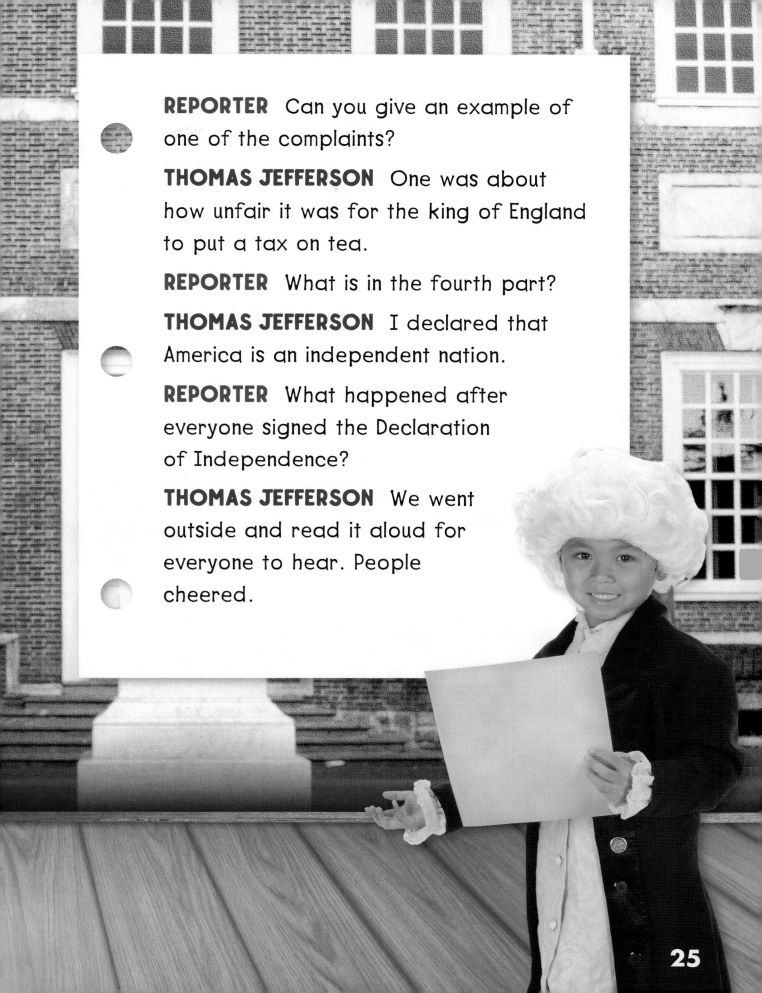

REPORTER Can you give an example of one of the complaints?

THOMAS JEFFERSON One was about how unfair it was for the king of England to put a tax on tea.

REPORTER What is in the fourth part?

THOMAS JEFFERSON I declared that America is an independent nation.

REPORTER What happened after everyone signed the Declaration of Independence?

THOMAS JEFFERSON We went outside and read it aloud for everyone to hear. People cheered.

First in War

REPORTER General Washington, you became the leader of the American army in 1775. What did you know about it at the time?

GEORGE WASHINGTON I knew how brave the men were. That gave me hope that we might win the war.

REPORTER You were once in the English army. How did that help you?

GEORGE WASHINGTON I learned that English soldiers are well trained, so I made rules for our men. Then we started training.

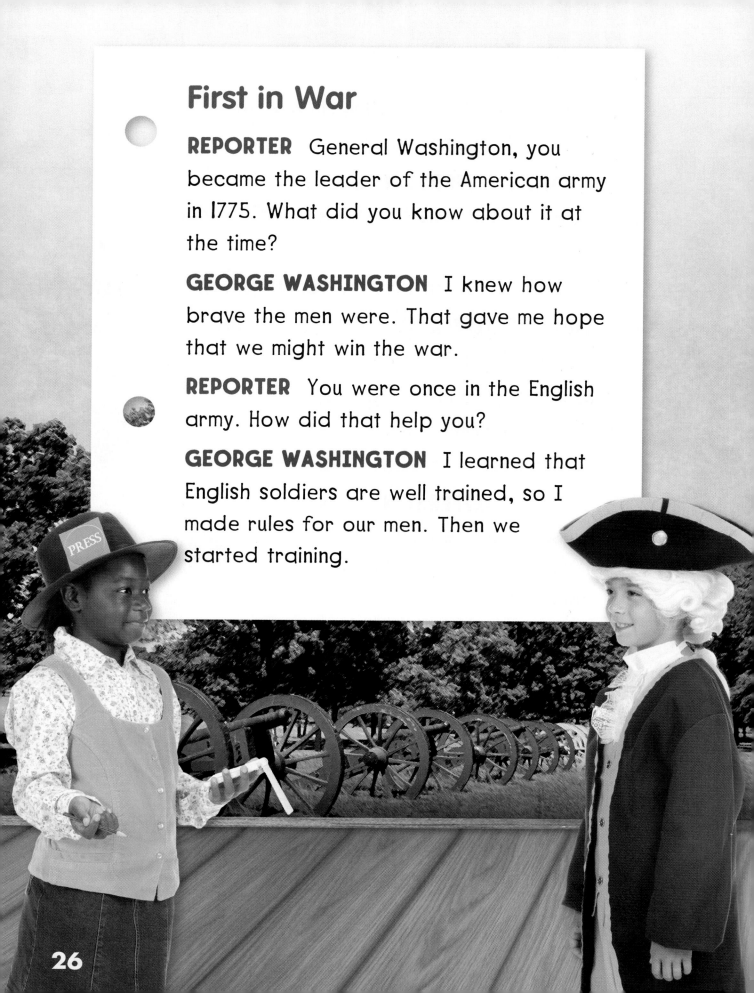

REPORTER General Washington, what will you do next, now that the war is over?

GEORGE WASHINGTON My plan is to send the English soldiers back to England. That way I will make sure that we stay a free and independent country forever.

Summary Many Americans helped America win its independence. Some fought in battles. Others helped in different ways.

Review

1. **What to Know** How did our country become independent?

2. **Vocabulary** What is a **revolution**?

3. ✏ **Write** Suppose you were a reporter during the American Revolution. Write a question you would ask one of the men from the interviews. Then write what you think his answer would be.

4. **Recall and Retell** Choose a person from one of the interviews. Tell what he did to help our country become independent.

Trustworthiness

Respect

Responsibility

Fairness

Caring

Patriotism

Why Character Counts

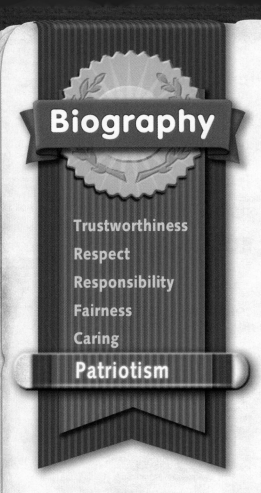

How did Benjamin Franklin show patriotism?

Benjamin Franklin

Benjamin Franklin was born in Boston, Massachusetts, in 1706. There were 17 children in his family. He started working when he was ten years old.

Benjamin Franklin became an inventor, a scientist, a leader, and a writer. He was famous for his sayings, such as "Well done is better than well said."

Most of all, Benjamin Franklin was a patriot. He loved his country.

Benjamin Franklin helped start the United States of America.

Benjamin Franklin helped write the Declaration of Independence.

Benjamin Franklin was one of the leaders in the colonies. At the time, England ruled the colonies. Benjamin Franklin worked to help the colonies become free. In 1776, he helped write the Declaration of Independence. During the American Revolution, he worked to get help from other countries. Later, he was one of the leaders who wrote the new country's Constitution. In all these ways, Benjamin Franklin showed his great love for his country.

GO ONLINE For more resources, go to
www.harcourtschool.com/ss1

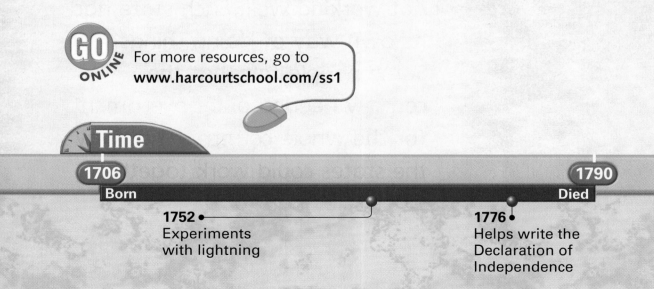

Time

1706			1790
Born			**Died**

1752 •
Experiments
with lightning

1776 •
Helps write the
Declaration of
Independence

 What to Know
Why was forming a government important for a new country?

Vocabulary
Bill of Rights

Forming a New Government

September 17, 1787, was the day the United States Constitution was signed. Constitution Day is just the beginning of the story of how 13 states became one nation.

One Nation

After the American Revolution, America was a free country. However, the government was not working well. Each state had its own way of doing things. Some people felt that the country needed one government for the whole country. That way the states could work together when they had to.

In 1787, leaders from 12 of the 13 states met in Philadelphia. Some of the leaders had met there before. They had signed the Declaration of Independence in Philadelphia.

This time the leaders went there to form a better government. They decided that what the country really needed was a new set of rules. One of those leaders was George Washington. He was one of the first to arrive.

Reading Check **What happened on September 17, 1787?**

The Constitution

It was hot that summer in Philadelphia, but the leaders could not open a window in the hall. They did not want anyone outside hearing what they were saying.

It was hard to get people to agree. Some states liked the idea of one government for the whole country. Others did not. The smaller states worried that all the power would go to the big states.

Reading Check **Why did the leaders at the meeting disagree?**

James Madison thought he could get the leaders to agree. He was one of the men who believed in a strong government. He talked to those who did not agree with him.

After a while, the leaders began to agree. One side gave up some things it wanted. The other side gave up some things it wanted. Finally, everyone agreed on a new set of rules for the government. It was called the Constitution.

The Bill of Rights

The people of most states liked the Constitution, but they still felt that something was missing. They wanted a **Bill of Rights** that would list the rights of every American.

James Madison and others promised to work on that list. That helped the states decide. In 1788, the states agreed to the new rules. The Constitution became the law. In 1789, the Bill of Rights was added. Now the country was really the United States of America.

(Reading Check) **What did the Bill of Rights add to the Constitution?**

The Constitution

We celebrate Constitution Day to remind us of our freedoms and our rights.

Summary After the American Revolution, the states agreed to a new set of rules for the government. It was called the Constitution. The Bill of Rights was soon added to the Constitution.

Review

① **What to Know** Why was forming a government important for a new country?

② **Vocabulary** What is the **Bill of Rights**? Why is it important?

③ ✏ **Write** Explain in one paragraph why it is important for the United States to have a Constitution.

④ **Cause and Effect** Why did the first government of the United States need to be changed?

Pioneers

What to Know
Why did Americans move west?

Vocabulary
pioneer

Early in our history, pioneers traveled west, hoping to find a better life. A **pioneer** is a person who first settles a new place.

One young pioneer girl is traveling with her family from Ohio to Oregon. This is her journal.

February 12, 1860

We have left our poor, rocky farm in Ohio forever. With luck, we will reach Oregon in the fall. Papa says the land there is so good for farming that we will be able to grow anything.

March 6, 1860

Today we reached the Missouri River and boarded a steamboat. Two other families are going to Oregon, but there are no girls my age. I miss my friend Laura.

March 15, 1860

We are in the busy town of Independence, Missouri. I help Mama buy supplies for the trip. There are no stores on the trail, so we have to carry everything we need. We buy flour, salt, dried fruit, and meat.

Guess what? Papa got me a puppy! I have named him Lookout.

June 18, 1860

We are on the Oregon Trail with sixteen other wagons. The trail seems to go on forever. Lookout barks at all the prairie dogs, and it makes me laugh. Playing with him helps me not to miss Laura so much.

July 14, 1860

Sometimes rainstorms soak all our bedding and clothes. We have to dry them in the sun. Other days are hot, and it's hard to find water.

There are many dangers, too. One time, Lookout saved me by barking at a rattlesnake! Papa says he earned his name that day.

October 28, 1860

We made it all the way to our new home in Oregon! We are building our house before the winter comes. Next spring we will plant crops in the rich soil.

I wrote a letter and sent it by Pony Express. The ponies and riders follow the same trail we came on. They will carry my letter all the way back to Ohio. Someday they may bring back a letter for me.

OREGON TRAIL

Missouri River

OREGON

OHIO

N

W   E

S

INDEPENDENCE

Our Pioneer
Journey

MAP SKILL In which direction did the pioneer family travel?

Summary A girl and her pioneer family make the long journey west. They leave their old home, hoping to find a better life.

Review

① **What to Know** Why did Americans move west?

② **Vocabulary** Describe the journey of the **pioneer** family.

③ **Activity** Make a diagram of the pioneer family's covered wagon. Include all the things you think they carried inside the wagon. Make sure to include pots, pans, and all other things needed for the trip. Don't forget Lookout!

④ **Recall and Retell** What were three of the challenges the pioneer family faced on the journey?

6 Native Americans Today

Native Americans were the first people to live in North America. Each Native American **tribe**, or group, had its own way of living.

A girl and her aunt on the Navajo Reservation at Nazlini, Arizona

Then settlers began to move west and form towns. The settlers forced most Native Americans to leave their lands. Many of them moved onto reservations. A **reservation** is land that is set aside for Native Americans to use.

Today there are many different Native American tribes living across the United States. Native Americans live on reservations, in cities, and on farms. They continue to speak their tribes' languages and follow their traditions.

Native American Cultures

Tribe	Clothing	Food	Shelter
Navajo			
Cherokee			
Lakota			
Iroquois			
Nez Perce			

The Navajo

Many Navajo people today live on a reservation that covers parts of Arizona, Utah, and New Mexico. It is the largest reservation in the United States.

Long ago, Navajo people made blankets from the wool of sheep. Today, Navajo artists still weave brightly colored blankets. Others make jewelry of silver and turquoise, a blue-green stone.

turquoise and silver belt buckle

Navajo weaver

Navajo blanket

The Cherokee

Most Cherokee people today live in Oklahoma. Long ago, most of the tribe was forced to move there from North Carolina.

A man named Sequoyah invented a system of writing for the Cherokee language. This helped the Cherokee write down their stories from long ago. Thanks to Sequoyah, those stories are still around today!

(Reading Check) **What did Sequoyah do?**

Sequoyah and the Cherokee writing system

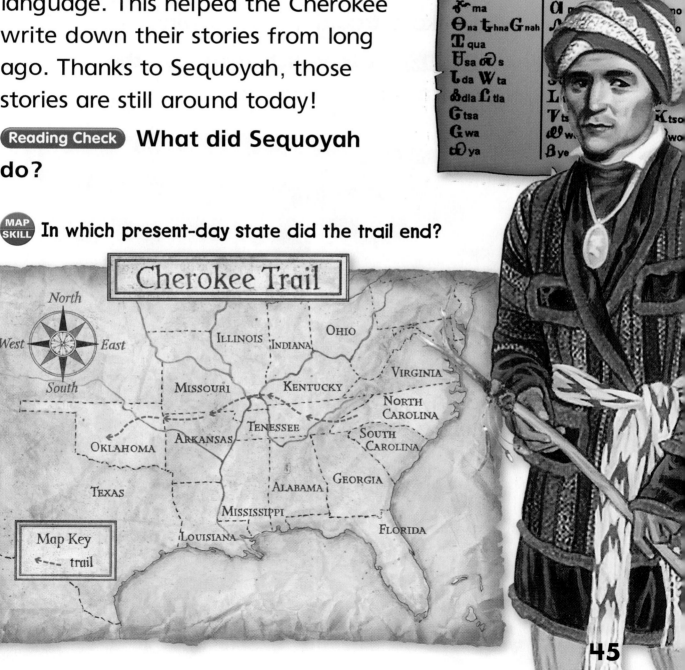

MAP SKILL In which present-day state did the trail end?

Cherokee Trail

Map Key
←--- trail

45

The Lakota

The Lakota tribe lives on reservations in North Dakota and South Dakota. They have parties for special occasions. At the parties, the hosts give gifts to all the guests. Long ago, gifts such as horses, clothing, and blankets were given away at these parties. It is part of Lakota tradition to be giving.

Reading Check **In which states do the Lakota have reservations?**

The Iroquois

The Iroquois tribe is made up of six separate tribes. The Iroquois call themselves the "people of the longhouse."

More than 400 years ago, the tribes came together under a law they called the Great Law of Peace. When the United States became a nation, it used ideas from the Iroquois tribe.

An Iroquois longhouse

"Roots have spread out from the Tree of the Great Peace, one to the north, one to the east, one to the south and one to the west. The name of these roots is The Great White Roots and their nature is Peace and Strength."

— The Great Law of Peace

The Nez Perce

The tribal flag of the Nez Perce shows the land of their reservation in Idaho. The river, salmon, eagle, and elk are all part of Nez Perce life. Can you find each of them on the flag?

The Nez Perce Reservation in Idaho

There are more than 500 Native American tribes today. They are all proud of their cultures and work to keep their traditions.

Summary Native Americans live all over the United States. They continue to keep their cultures and traditions from the past.

Review

1. **What to Know** What are some of the Native American groups living in the United States today?

2. **Vocabulary** What is a **reservation**?

3. **Write** Choose a tribe from the chart on page 43. Write a paragraph about the food, shelter, and clothing of that tribe.

4. **Cause and Effect** When settlers began moving west, what happened to Native Americans?

What to Know
How did the people living in Asia long ago affect our lives today?

Vocabulary
temple
pagoda

Asia in the Past

More than 5,000 years ago, people all over Asia began to live together in groups. Their inventions, ideas, and art are now very old, but they are still part of our lives today.

India

Long ago, two different ways of believing began in India. They are called Hinduism and Buddhism. These two religions have now spread all over the world. New tools in math and science were also first developed in India.

People who follow Hinduism believe Ganesha can help them solve their problems. Today, people who follow Hinduism have Ganesha festivals.

The Buddha started Buddhism in India long ago. He traveled across the land, teaching people his ideas about being good.

Numbers

Long Ago	ο	۱	۲	۳	૪	५	६	७	८	९
Today	0	1	2	3	4	5	6	7	8	9

A new way of writing numbers was invented long ago in India.

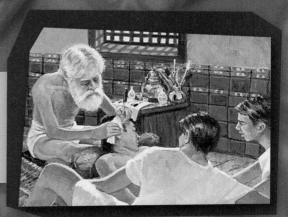

Indian doctors invented ways to keep people from getting sick. They helped people live healthier lives.

China

People traveled from India to China. They brought ideas from India with them. When Buddhism came to China, the Chinese built temples. A **temple** is a building in which people follow their beliefs.

CHINA

Today, people can still visit temples in China that were built thousands of years ago.

More than 7,000 clay soldiers were found in a cave in China. They show what Chinese soldiers wore.

People traveled from other countries to trade with the Chinese. Chinese goods were traded all over the world. Many things we use today were invented long ago in China.

The Chinese made the world's first paper and found a way to print books.

They invented fireworks.

They dried plant leaves to make tea.

They invented the first mechanical clock.

Japan

Long ago, many inventions, ideas, and art traveled from China to Japan. Over time, the Japanese developed their own unique culture.

JAPAN

The Japanese built pagodas. A **pagoda** is a building with many stories. It is often used as a temple.

They invented their own written language.

They made pots out of clay.

Our Lives Today

Ways of living from long ago in Asia are still part of life there today. Inventions, ideas, and art of Asia's past can be found all over the world. What we learn about Asia's past helps us understand how we live today.

Summary People who lived in Asia long ago invented things, started new ideas, and made art. Many of their inventions, ideas, and artwork are part of our lives today.

Review

1 **What to Know** How did the people living in Asia long ago affect our lives today?

2 **Vocabulary** What is a **temple**?

3 **Activity** Make a poster about one country in Asia. Show things that people have made there.

4 **Main Idea and Details** Name three countries in Asia. Name one thing we use today that came from each country long ago.

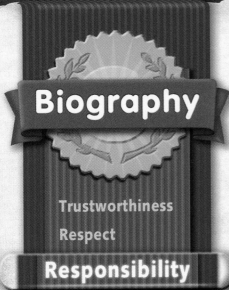

Trustworthiness

Respect

Responsibility

Fairness

Caring

Patriotism

Why Character Counts

How did Marco Polo show responsibility?

Marco Polo

Marco Polo was born in 1254 in what is now Venice, Italy. His father and uncle were merchants. They often went to faraway lands to buy and sell goods. In 1271, they took Marco with them on one of their trips.

The trip was long and difficult. Marco and his father and uncle traveled by sea and over land. They crossed hot, dry deserts. They climbed high, cold mountains. At last, after four years, they reached China.

Marco Polo wrote about his travels in Asia.

Marco Polo traveled from his home in Venice to eastern Asia

The emperor, or ruler, of China liked Marco Polo. He gave him many important jobs. One time, the emperor sent him to explore other lands. Finally, after many years, Marco Polo and his family went back to Venice.

A few years later, Marco Polo wrote a book about his travels. He was once asked if his stories were true or made up. He answered, "I have not told half of what I saw." His stories made people want to see the world.

GO ONLINE For more resources, go to www.harcourtschool.com/ss1

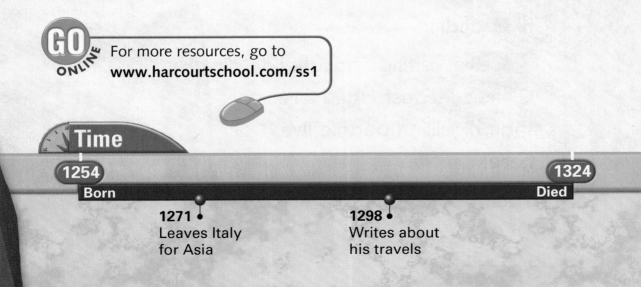

Time

1254 Born
1324 Died
1271 Leaves Italy for Asia
1298 Writes about his travels

Asia Today

What to Know
How has Asia changed since long ago?

Vocabulary

agriculture

Asia is the largest continent. It takes up the most land. More people live in Asia than on any other continent in the world!

China, India, and Japan are three countries in Asia. The cultures, or ways of life, in these countries are thousands of years old. If you traveled to Asia today, what might you see?

Cities in Asia

Hi Grandma,

We're visiting Shanghai, China's largest city. More than 12 million people live here!

Zach

Mumbai, India
BOAT TOURS

Dear Morgan,

Mumbai, India, is a huge city on seven islands. Today Mom and I saw a movie being made. They make lots of movies here!

Dad

Hi Sam,

Tokyo is the largest city in the world. It's so busy! Tomorrow we will take a bullet train to see more of Japan.

Natalie

BULLET TRAIN TO TOKYO

Famous Landmarks in Asia

Hi Grandma,

Many years ago, the people of China built the Great Wall. They wanted to keep strangers out of China. Today, people from all over the world can visit the Great Wall.

Zach

GREAT WALL OF CHINA

Dear Morgan,

The Taj Mahal was built in India 350 years ago. A thousand elephants carried the marble, stone, and jewels to build it!

Love,
Dad

FABULOUS Mt. Fuji

Hi Sam,

Mt. Fuji is a volcano in Japan. Many Japanese artists have painted it. People come from all over the world to climb Mt. Fuji.

Natalie

Land and Jobs in Asia

Hi Grandma,

In the past, most Chinese people used the land for **agriculture**, or farming. Today, some still grow rice and other crops. Many others work in factories like this. They make toys, clothes, and other goods sold all over the world.

Zach

CHINA

INDIA

Dear Morgan,

As in the past, India still has many farmers. They grow the most wheat and tea of any country in the world. Many other people in India work with technology. These women have jobs working with computers.

Dad

Dear Sam,

   A small number of farmers still grow rice in Japan. Most Japanese people live in cities, though. Yesterday I saw a factory where they make cars and another where they make computers.

Natalie

Japan

Asian Culture

Hi Grandma,

Chinese people still eat with chopsticks, just as they did long ago. All the people at the table share the different foods.

Zach

Dear Morgan,

In India, some women and girls still wear saris. The saris are made from brightly colored cloth.

Dad

Dear Sam,

In traditional Japanese homes, people take off their shoes before entering. The floors are covered with straw mats called tatami.

Natalie

In the modern cities of Asia, cars, skyscrapers, and computers are common. However, you can still find a culture that began long, long ago.

SHANGHAI

Summary The Asian countries of China, India, and Japan are thousands of years old. They are now modern countries, but old traditions are still part of their cultures today.

Review

① **What to Know** How has Asia changed since long ago?

② **Vocabulary** What are some kinds of **agriculture** in Asian countries today?

③ **Write** Write a postcard to a friend. Tell something you would like to see or do in Asia.

④ **Compare and Contrast** Make lists of ways life in Asia today is similar to and different from the way it was long ago.

Review and Test Prep

Vocabulary

Choose the word that matches the description.

Word Bank

artifact
(p. 8)
trade
(p. 13)
reservation
(p. 43)
temple
(p. 52)
agriculture
(p. 62)

① an area of land that is set aside for Native Americans to use

② a building in which people follow their beliefs

③ farming

④ to exchange goods

⑤ any object that people have made, especially from long ago

Facts and Main Ideas

⑥ Who were the Mound Builders?

⑦ Why did the pioneers move west?

⑧ What was the Boston Tea Party?

⑨ What is the Bill of Rights?

   A. a book about the Constitution

   B. the name of a country

   C. a list of the rights of all Americans

   D. a statement declaring independence

66

⑩ Which American leader was also an inventor, a scientist, and a writer?

    A. Thomas Jefferson   **B.** Paul Revere

    C. George Washington   **D.** Benjamin Franklin

Critical Thinking

⑪ Why is it important to learn about people long ago?

⑫ **Make It Relevant** How would your life be different without the Bill of Rights?

Hands-On Activity

Create a Mural Choose one of the people, events, or places described in this book. Draw a mural about it. Show the important details about that person, event, or place.